Rub-down transfer book

The Wild Garden

Illustrated by Bethan Janine

Designed by Mary Cartwright & Emily Beevers
Edited by Felicity Brooks

You'll find the transfers at the front of the book.
There are tips on how to use them at the back.

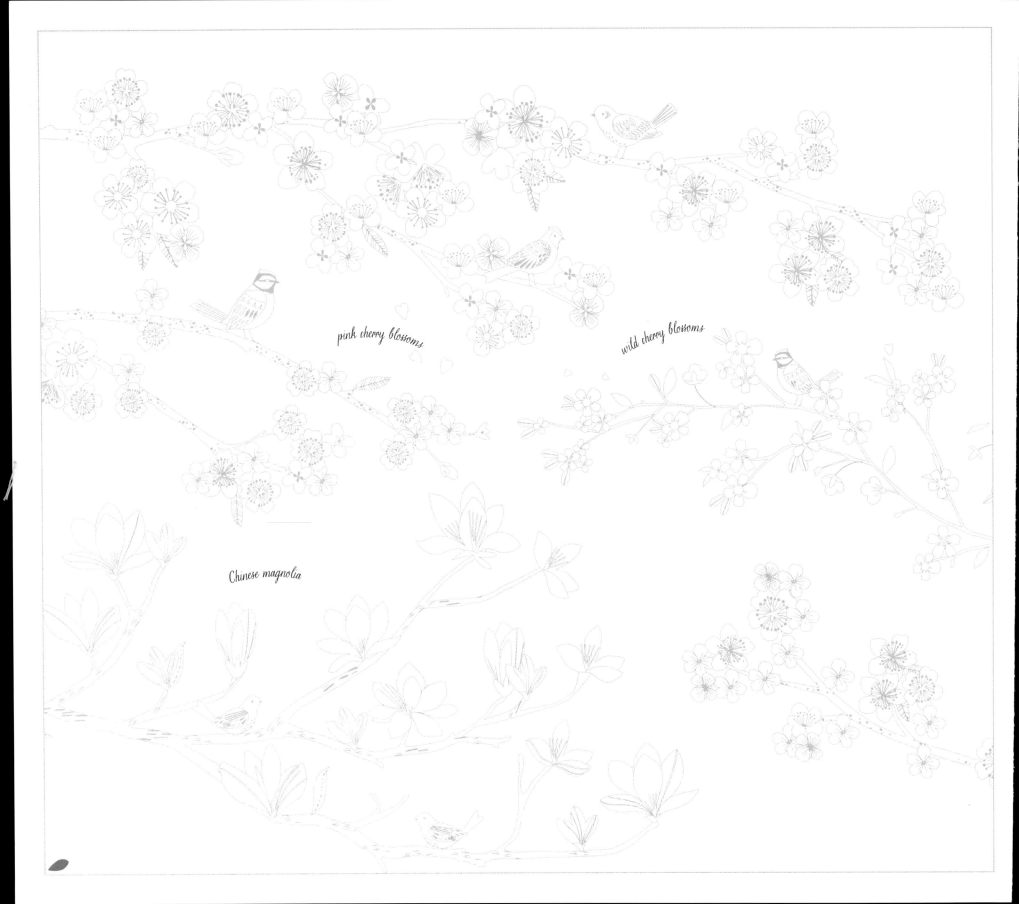

pink cherry blossoms

wild cherry blossoms

Chinese magnolia

Spring Blossoms

painted lady

small copper

buddleia flower

peacock

red admiral

common blue

tortoiseshell

brimstone

comma

Butterfly Garden

At the Pond

cow parsley

damselfly

bumblebee

knapweed

burnet moth

common poppy

field scabious

meadow rue

Summer Meadow

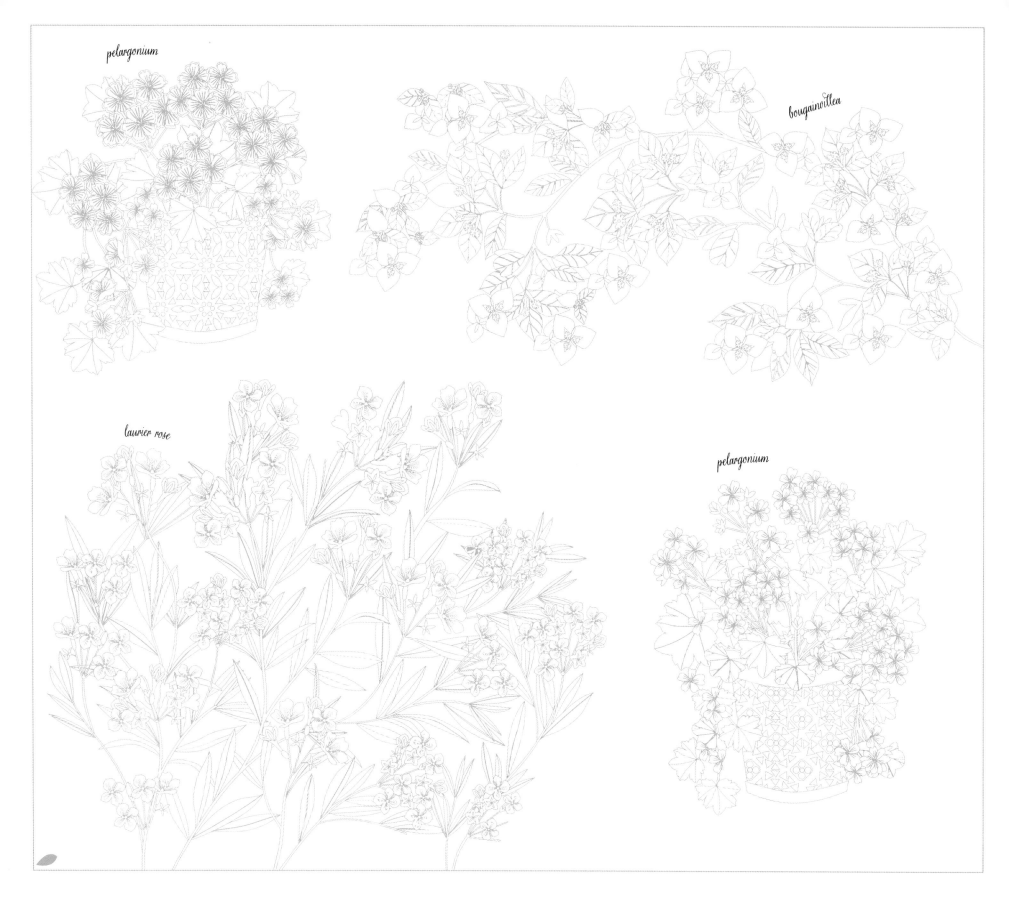

pelargonium

bougainvillea

laurier rose

pelargonium

Mediterranean Garden

alba rose

nasturtium

hollyhock

larkspur

Grecian rose or geum

lupin

sweet william

forget-me-not

Cottage Garden

orchid

bromeliads

hummingbird

heliconia

Tropical Garden

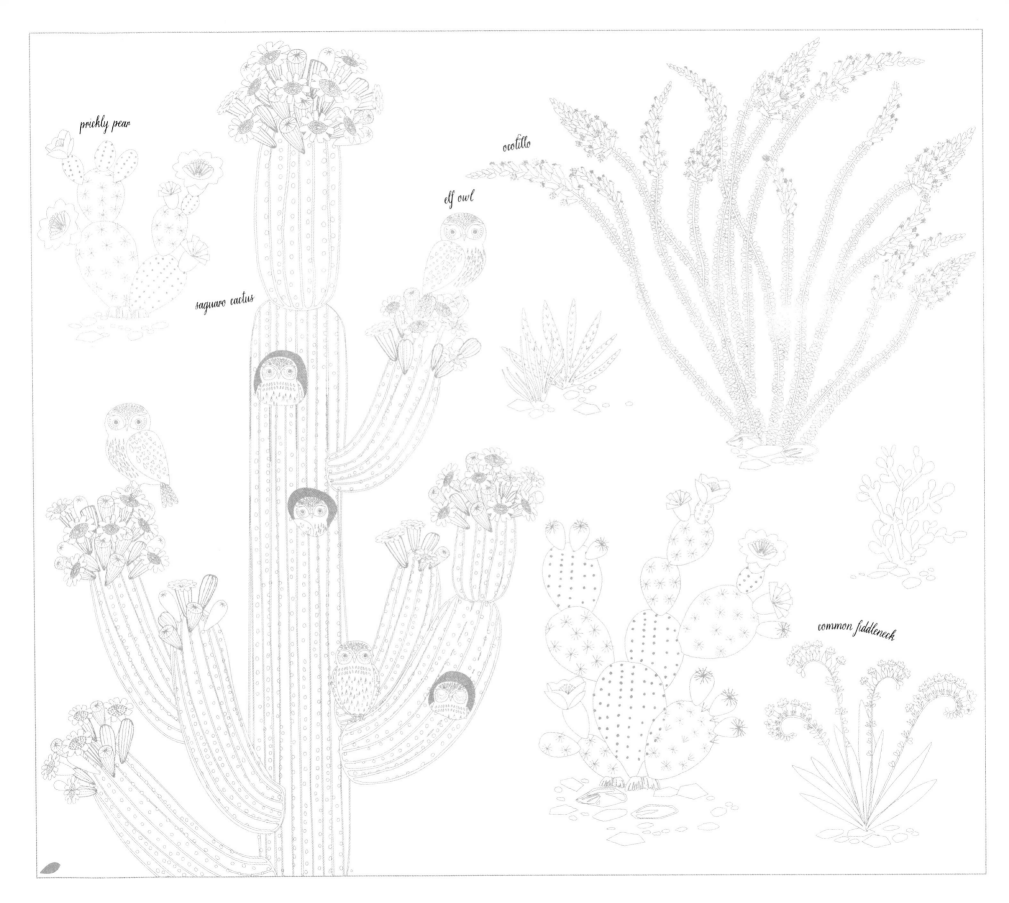

prickly pear

ocotillo

elf owl

saguaro cactus

common fiddleneck

Cactus Garden

swallowtail

sea thrift

valerian

California poppy

cotton lavender

sea kale

sea holly

On the Seashore

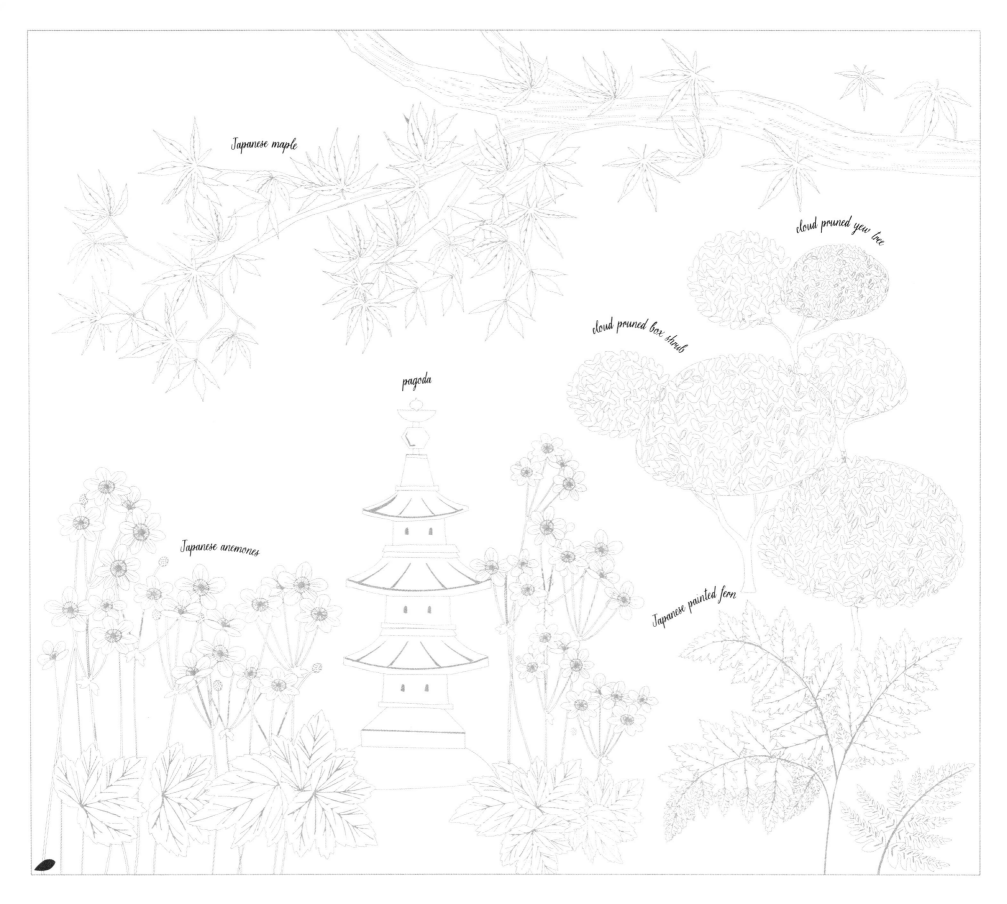

Japanese maple

cloud pruned yew tree

cloud pruned box shrub

pagoda

Japanese anemones

Japanese painted fern

Japanese Garden

holly

rowan berries

rose hips

Jerusalem sage

teasel

In the Winter

How to use this book

To create some gorgeous gardens, you'll need a ballpoint pen or a pencil to add the rub-down transfers to the right-hand pages of this book. You can use crayons or felt-tip pens to decorate the left-hand pages.

Using the transfers

Take the transfer sheets out of their pocket and find the one with the leaf symbol that exactly matches the symbol on the pages you want to work on. (Some sheets contain the transfers for two gardens.)

To use the transfers, position one of the little pictures over the place you want it to go in the garden.

Scribble all over it firmly with a pencil or ballpoint pen, taking care not to touch the pictures around it.

When you have completely covered the transfer, gently lift off the transfer sheet.

First published in 2016 by Usborne Publishing Ltd., Usborne House, 83-85 Saffron Hill, London EC1N 8RT, England. Printed in China.

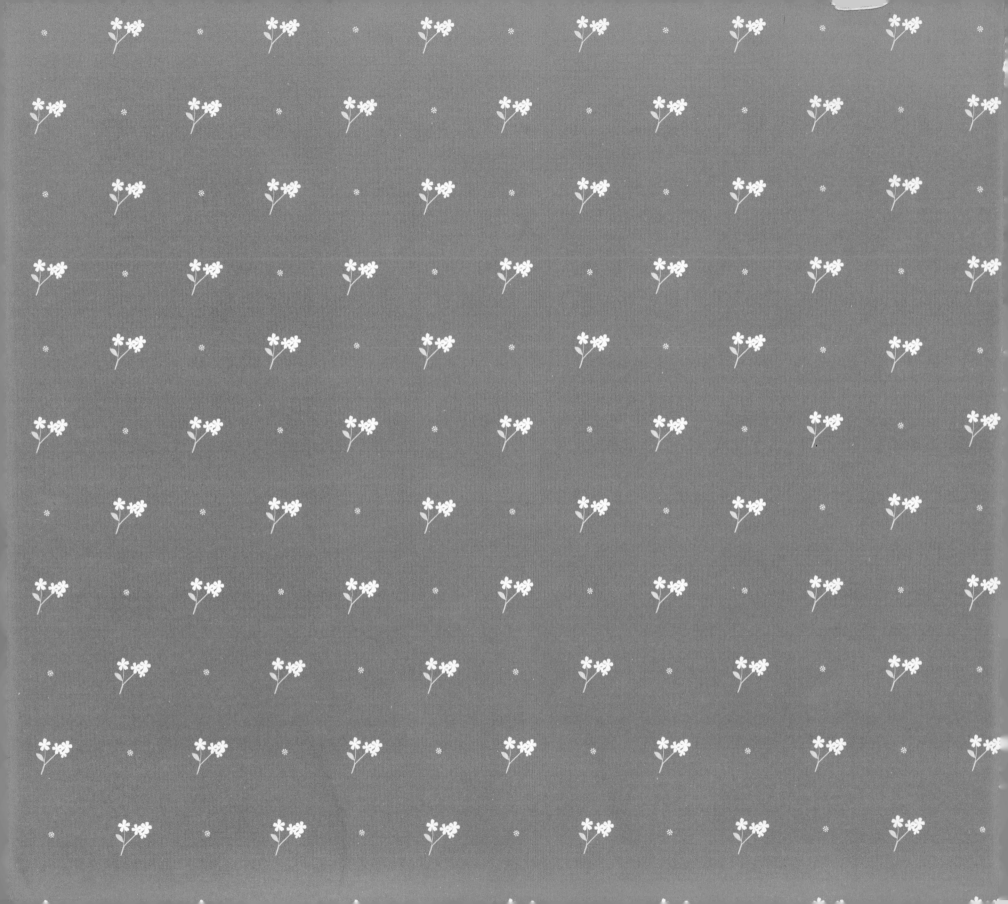